MY TRUMPETS ARE SOUNDING!

PROPHESY! PROPHESY!

AS GIVEN TO

JERRY WILLIS

DEDICATION

To Jesus, my life!

To my wife, Vivien, the love of my life, and the one with whom I shared my happiest years

To my children, grandchildren, and great grandchildren whom I love

To my dear friends whose company I enjoy

CONTENTS

THIS BOOK IS DIVIDED INTO EIGHT SECTIONS:

PROPHECY

"For prophecy never had its origin in the will of man, but men spoke from God as they were carried along by the Holy Spirit!" -2 Pet. 1:21

"Follow the way of love and eagerly desire spiritual gifts, especially the gift of prophecy." -1 Cor. 14:1

"Worship God, for the testimony of Jesus is the Spirit of Prophecy." -Rev 19:10

"There shall be a major change in My people when they recognize that the Gift of Prophesy is *the pure love of Me*, the Christ, and receive it. They will begin to realize that whatever circumstances they are in, I Am still with them:" -*My Trumpets are Sounding* page 61

ACKNOWLEDGMENTS

THE SPIRIT OF TRUTH, JESUS CHRIST: For giving me these words.

VIVIEN WILLIS, MY WIFE: For transcribing my hand written messages into print, for organizing them into a book, and for her love and encouragement.

KAREN RANDALL, A DEAR FRIEND for working many hours to proof my manuscript

DR. PAUL AND DR. FAYE RICHARDSON: Founders of *The Spirit of Truth Institute*, where I received my Doctor of Christology Degree, who shared their time and resources to bless our ministry.

FORWARD

"For My thoughts are not your thoughts; neither are your ways My ways, saith the Lord. For as the heavens are higher than the earth, so are My ways higher than your ways, and My thoughts than your thoughts." -Isa. 55:8-9

"The messages in this book were given to me by the Lord. They are not my thoughts. I do not even think or talk this way. I promise you, the reader, if you will ask without prejudice, the Heavenly Father will show the truth of them. If there are errors or mistakes, it is because they come through an imperfect vessel as myself." –Jerry Willis

MY TRUMPETS ARE CALLING "AMERICA!"

PART I

PROPHETIC WORDS GIVEN

JERRY WILLIS

PROPHESY! PROPHESY!

1. AMERICA, OH, AMERICA

The Spirit says:

I have warned you of the enemy within, and you heard Me not. Now comes a time like no other!

This land is undergoing a trial, and out of this trial shall come renewal. For this land is a precious land unto Me. I will that all who live here shall serve Me or they shall be swept off.

Stay your heart on Me, America! For the wisdom of the world is perishing, and all the learned that will not hear Me shall perish. I Am He who has ruled from the foundation of the world. There is good and evil. Choose you this day which you will serve. -Josh. 24:5

I see many who still love Me; therefore, I will save them from the destruction to come.

Remember, oh, remember, you did not choose Me; I have chosen you. -John 15:16

It is the same this day as in the past. Those who would vault themselves up shall fall, and the ones you think not shall be raised by My Hand.

I Am the Light and the Life of the world, and without Me all is darkness. -John 8:12

Look into your hearts, My people, and tell Me what you see there. Have the evil things of this world overcome you? You fight against others who are "Believers" and think you do a good work. You believe you are wise and know Me. You have much to learn. I do not fight those who believe, but I strengthen them! I help them grow strong in faith.

I want you to soften your hearts toward all others and think yourself foolish for believing that you are right and they are wrong.

Look at Me, My children, and know Who and What I Am. For I Am the First and the Last, and besides Me there is no other. -Isa. 44:6

Your world I have created, and I know all that takes place. Fear not, for I Am with you always. -Luke 12:32

Even so,

Amen.

In a very short time I will fulfill all My promises, and the things you shall see will be glorious in your eyes. They are foretold by My prophets of old. They remain with Me.

Men may say these words are not of Me, for My Words do not uphold what men believe to be true. If you do not ask, you will not receive. The truth is not hard to find if you really seek. It will be given to you! Ask Me, for I send none away. Seek Me, for I Am He who upholds.

Listen not to the voice of men, no matter how personable they are or how much they sound as if they have My authority.

My authority is always filled with My Spirit and uplifts, even those I chastise. I read the heart, and I cannot be fooled by anyone or anything. There are many who play at being holy, but only One is Holy! Bend your knees, My children, and learn that I do not misunderstand the hearts of those who call on Me.

My small ones, I have great compassion for you. I will always be close to you, even until the end comes. Fear not what man can do, but fear what God can do.

Blessed is he who hears and obeys My Voice. My love is with you always, and I shall cleanse every stain if you will trust in Me only!

There are those among you whom I have called, and there are some that I have not called. This should be easy to see if you will hear Me. Those who speak in My place and make their calling above the calling of others, might do well to ask of Me. For I told My apostles, "It should not be so among you." -Matt.20:25-28 But rather, "When you are converted, strengthen the brethren." -Luke 22:32 If this be not the case, follow not that voice, for I have not changed. I am the same today as yesterday.-Heb. 13:8 Do not listen, if I Am changed!

My little children, you are precious to Me, and I know

the errors which are among you. They can easily be corrected if your heart is not hardened.

What would you that I do? I do not put new wine in old bottles, for they would both be lost. I will and already have begun new things. -Matt. 9:17

My people meet often and seek Me, for it is I they wish to follow. Why is this so troubling to some? Do they not know Me?

I am not bound by the traditions of man, regardless of man's assumptions that I can only be what man wants. I never have been under man's control!

Read your scriptures, and you will know Me. You must come to Me with full purpose of heart or I cannot receive you.

You who are bound and wish to be free, come and learn of Me from Me. Open your heart and your ears and your eyes that you might see, hear, and feel Me.

All things are possible with Me, and nothing good is possible without Me! -Luke 12:32

Fear not, My children, all things are as they should be, and they will be forever more.

Amen.

Oh, My people, I would that you understand that My love is endless. I love all My creation, and I do not create things that are of no value. I would, My people, that you try to find the good things in life so that your heart can remain soft toward others. I would that you believe all things that are good, for if they are good, they are from Me. I would that you judge only between good and evil and choose the good.

Remember that I Am Holy! I will always remain Holy. Therefore, wherever I Am is Holy. -1Pet. 1:16

Nothing I say to you is meant to give you power over others, but it is to bring all who will to Me

I will give My blessing to each and everyone who opens the door of his heart and mind to Me. I want all to turn from that which keeps themselves from Me. I have given all things necessary for you to follow Me. I say, come unto Me, My little ones, for the night is fast approaching, and time will not wait. I have loved you from the beginning, and I still love you.

Hear My Words. Search your heart today, and cleanse all thought of "self" for My sake. -Matt.16:24 Take your cross and follow Me to a place of peace and rest where you shall be protected and raised up as a calf in a stall. -Malachi 4:2 I have naught but good to offer you, My children, if you will hear Me this day.

Peace be with you. My peace I give unto you—not as the world gives, but a strength of peace in your heart give I unto you that you shall know where you belong.

You who hear, come and drink from My Living Water and taste of wine and milk bought without money and without price. -Isa. 55:1 Come, My little ones, and live.

These words I speak to your spirit that you will understand later as time moves forward.

I say unto you, love is the answer, for love is the enduring of all things, even as it was in the beginning, is now, and shall ever be.

Amen and Amen!

2. NATION IN PERIL

The Spirit says:

O, son of man, I hold out My Hand to My ministers, but they hear Me not. I say unto them, "Judge not by your traditions."

You, whom I have chosen, are not humble before Me. You, whom I have chosen, fail to ask of Me. You, whom I have chosen, are going your own way. You, whom I have chosen, judge by your tradition and put heavy burdens on My people. You whom I have chosen to loose all bonds. You, whom I have chosen, did not choose Me. I speak to you in My way, and you refuse Me. My people are in bondage today because you have gone your own way.

If you will turn unto Me, I will turn unto you. Look into your own hearts, and tell me what you see there. Then you will hear Me.

Your nation is in great peril, and you know it not. Secret combinations of old are at work, and things are not what they seem.

Fear not. Neither let your heart be troubled. -John 14:1

I tell you of this so you may know before it comes to pass. All things are known, and there is nothing that is not known.

If your nation and My people turn their hearts to Me, I will heal them. I will be their God, and they will be My people. -Jer. 24:7 For I Am He who was born of woman, suffered, died, and arose on the third day. I Am alive evermore.

My People, you must look unto Me, not the world, for time grows ever shorter. I will not strive with man forever. Any who will hear, let them hear.

Any who will ask of Me, will I tell, for nothing do I in secret. All is done in the open.

Soon all will know that I Am, for I will work among the children of men a "marvelous work and a wonder." And blessed are you if you believe Me, that I Am. -Isa. 29:14

My people will arise as cream comes to the top. Those who will hear, let them hear.

Look into your hearts, My people, and cast away those things that are of the world.

Judge yourself this day, and I will heal your wounds and make you whole. I will ease your pain and burdens, and you will prosper, for I Am mighty to save. I Am the First and the Last, and besides Me there is no other! -Isa. 44:6

Heed not the words of the world, but heed My words.

The wisdom of the wise is about to perish and the knowledge of the learned to vanish. -Isa.29:14 They will not have answers for what is about to happen, for they see through the eyes of man.

My people will see and hear My word.

Argue not with any man, nor make it a point of contention. If they ask of Me with open hearts, I will reason with them.

Remember, oh, remember, You did not choose Me, but I have chosen you!

If you love Me, keep My sayings.

3. AMERICA, A CHOICE LAND

Prophesy this to My people:

Your land is a choice land. I have truly blessed it. Now because your government has led the people far from Me and has begun an abomination against Me, I shall stand against it!

The troubles of your nation have been from without. Now they will be from within. Because they have set father against son and mother against daughter, this abomination shall not stand!

America, you were to be a light unto the world. You were given many blessings from Me. Now will I cause you to suffer that which was foretold. If they (your government) will not hearken to My words and come to Me with a humble spirit, I will confuse and frustrate all their doings.

My people, fear not! -Luke 12:32 Take up no weapons against anyone. Place your trust in Me.

Come close to one another. Follow My words that all may be well with you. Pray often and I will hear you.

Those who are now in the seats of power have turned

from Me and harden their hearts against My people. They believe that I know not. Their secrets are an open book.

Endeavor to cause peace among My people. Many there will be who need help. Things must come to pass that My word be fulfilled, for all of mankind must know that I Am.

The Kingdom is your goal. Help in any way that you can to show people how to live in peace and harmony. Lo, I Am with you always. Be of a joyful heart, My people, for I find great love in you—love for Me—and I will protect and defend My people.

Fear not what man does! Fear only the Lord. If you will be obedient to Me, I will deliver you.

But if you harden your hearts and hear not My words, then you will have cause for great fear. The time of harvest is ever nearer. Come now to the open door, and do not look back, for the world is full of iniquity. I will cleanse you of all your sins and make you spotless before My Father if you will follow Me!

Thus saith the Lord God,

Amen.

4. THE VINEYARD, PART I

[Note: My wife Vivien and I were traveling somewhere when the Holy Spirit came upon me powerfully, and the Lord began to speak to me. Vivien wrote the message as it was given to me. The words came as quickly as they could be written down.]

The Spirit says:

What more could I have done in My vineyard than I have done? When I called, there was none to hear. When I spoke, none would listen. Therefore, this time is the last time I will call if they refuse to hear. It is the last time I will call upon them. This is the last time!

I have dug about the roots of the tree. I have dunged it, for I have given all. I have given My blood. This is the last time.

There are those who will say I have not spoken, for they will not understand My words. They see Me as they wish I was, but I Am He who has created them, and I know their hearts, and I know their thoughts even before they think them. I have rent the veil for all who will look upon Me with unfettered eyes. See Me as I truly Am, for My bowels are full of mercy for those who will.

There are those who call My people many names, but My people are of one heart. They refuse to bend the knee to man. They are they for whom I have died. They are they who gladly open their hearts and bend their knees to Me, for I love them, and they follow Me. They hear My Voice, and another voice they will not hear.

Amen.

5. THE VINEYARD-PART II

[Note: Later, the same day that I had received Part I of this message, I told my wife, "I need to go back over the message because the Holy Spirit has let me know that I have missed some of the words." I was told the Lord would give them to me later.]

The Holy Spirit came upon me again. These are the rest of the words:

My people, I have such love for thee. I have stood in the furrow of time. I have pledged My undying love for thee. Can thou not now hear Me?

The things I ask of thee, are they too great? Can you not feel the pleading of your Father's heart for thee? Will you not turn your heart to Me? Will you continue to stand against your brothers and sisters for the sake of traditions, even as your forefathers have done?

I love the whole of My creation. I wish for all to see the errors of man and to forsake their past and follow Me.

I say this unto all who will:

"Come unto Me that I may give you rest. Be baptized

27

that I may make you clean. Receive the Holy Ghost that I may reveal My True Self unto thee."

Is this too hard? I call now. Will you answer?

Amen.

6. FEAR NOT THE ASSYRIAN

Thus saith the Spirit:

I have told you before, and I tell you again, "Fear not the Assyrian." -Isa. 10:24 For as I live and breathe, he shall not come near thee! I the Lord God hath commanded it.

The scales of darkness shall begin to fall from My peoples' eyes, and they shall begin to see clearly "Who" and "What" I Am and what I stand for. Then the teaching of men will lose its power over them, and I shall reign in their hearts forever.

Amen.

7. I BROUGHT FORTH

Prophesy this to My people:

In the year 1776, I brought forth upon this land the beginnings of a nation—a nation unlike any other, a refuge for the oppressed of the world.

Now I have blessed this land above all lands, and I have cursed it above all that the wicked shall not long abide. My people will rise in this land. They must come unto Me, saith the Lord.

I call all!

Those who answer, I will bless that they be not blotted out. Those who refuse will be cut off. I have spoken it!

This nation must fulfill its obligation to the poor of this land and of the world. A time soon comes when all the ancient prophecies will be in effect. For the prophecies of old are not changed. When the people ripen in iniquity, and are fully ripe, then comes sudden destruction. At no time have I changed. Man teaches change, but I do not change.

All that I have spoken will be fulfilled.

Watch always, for I come soon. Trust the Lord your God, and wait upon Him.

Blessed is he who hears and pleas for the repentance of this nation, for the prayers of the oppressed have not gone unheard. They are not wasted. My people, you must draw nearer. Time is ever shorter.

Thus saith your Lord, Your God, even Jesus Christ.

Amen.

8. MY CHILDREN, WEEP

The Spirit says:

I ask you to weep. Cry for My beautiful land. Cry in your hearts and your souls for the fair ones who shall be lost. Cry for the terrible ones who shall suffer. I have cried for them, and I now ask that you, My children, cry for them.

My beautiful land is being overrun, and the beautiful things are being destroyed!

Be not afraid of the Assyrian, for he shall not come near thee, My children. But weep for the ones who will not hear Me. Walk in peace with your fellowman, and know that I Am God. -Ps. 46:10

Broken hearts I mend, contrite spirits I repair, and tears I dry. Follow Me, My children, and know that I love you. It may seem to thee a strange thing that I ask. I remember to cry for the things that make you sad, and I make them better for your sake. Can you not feel, for My sake, the sadness I feel for the lost?

How beautiful on the mountains are the feet of those who

can share a portion of My peace. Peace be upon you. My peace I give to you. These are promises I will always keep. -Isa. 52:7

Hear now, My children, that your world is changing, and things are not going to be the same. Many will refuse to believe the change and say it is of the devil, but I tell you it is of Me.

Much time was allotted to man, and much time has passed away. Soon the truth of things will begin to be known again, for they cannot keep back My Light forever.

Men have heard but did not understand. Some have made a pretense of understanding, but they do not know of themselves. I say, look about you. See all the things that have changed, and know it is just the beginning.

I will not leave you to perish in the dark. I Am He who brings Light into the darkness, and soon the world will not be able to deny Me any longer. Pray for one another, and pray for My beautiful land.

I Am with you always.

Amen.

9. WEEP AGAIN

[Note: On this day I was overcome with a sense of sadness that caused me to weep. This had happened several times recently. I did not understand why, as I am a very happy person.]

Suddenly, the Holy Spirit spoke to me: "Did I not ask that you weep for My fair ones which shall be lost?"

[Note: Then I realized my sadness was about the many sons and daughters of America (the precious land, a choice spot, blessed above all others) who are being lost. I do weep for them, but my tears are not important. What is important is God's sadness at the loss of even one of His fair ones! Oh, my brothers and sisters, I would desire that you take a moment to reflect on what this nation was and what it now is! Surely you can see why God asks us to weep for His fair ones who shall be lost.]

Oh, My children, hear Me, says the Lord:

I extend still My arms to you. If you will repent and return unto Me, I will heal your land, for it is precious unto Me. I will not allow destruction to come upon those who love Me!

Open your spiritual eyes and ears, and hear and see Me.

35

And I will bring you to Me, a place of rest and resurrection of spirit, so that you may prosper once again.

If you will not, I will not break My covenant. You have to choose who you will follow. Amen.

Oh, My children, you surely must choose. I have taken upon Myself the sin of the world. I have given all for you, My children.

Now hear My words:

The blessing I give to you is Eternal Life if you will return to Me with all your heart, might, and strength. There are many great things to be given to you, My children.

Can you not feel My presence?

Can you not hear My words?

Will you not be freed from your bonds?

Choose whom you will spend eternity with: My enemy or Me. I offer you peace and love, and I Am able to deliver you. What is to come is of love, not hate.

All things are as they should be.

Amen and Amen!

10. I SHALL SHAKE THIS LAND

[Note: I had tossed and turned most of the night because of a storm. There had been a lot of thunder and lightning.]

The Spirit says:

You say that you had a troubled night. You say that you were not able to sleep because of all the thunder and lightning? I walked across My land last night. I looked in sadness upon My beautiful land, for all the things that should be done are yet not done. And all the things that I would do for you, My people, I cannot do because of your unbelief.

There are a determined number of days, for the evil has possessed your land. When those days are accomplished, evil will end!

For this is My choice land, above all other lands, and I will have a people who will hear My Voice and recognize that I do no evil ever! For I Am Holy, and I love all of My creation. And all that I do is for the good of My creation.

It is but a short time and I will come.

Amen.

Prophesy to My people:

I shall stretch forth My upon this land, and other lands, across this nation, and other nations, until I cover the whole world. And I shall begin to shake in diverse places that you know not of.

The shaking shall be light at first, but it will grow in size and intensity. For all things that can be shaken will be shaken, for the bonds that hold My people must be broken! My people must be free from the bonds and chains that hold them captive that they know not of. Therefore, I will shake until all things that are not on a firm foundation will fall. -Heb. 12:26-27

I Am the Foundation, and all that stands on Me will stand. Fear not, for the stumbling blocks and the dark scales on My peoples' eyes must be removed. I Am He who created you from before the foundation of time. I will fulfill all My words.

Amen.

MY SHOFAR IS SOUNDING "ISRAEL!"

PART II

PROPHETIC WORDS GIVEN

JERRY WILLIS

PROPHESY! PROPHESY!

11. THE SOUNDING OF THE SHOFAR

A VISION

[Note: I went to bed and while lying there, I heard a sound. I wondered, "What is that?" Then I heard it again and recognized it was a single trumpet. Then I heard a shofar sound. The sound of the ram's horn took me right into a vision.]

I was sitting on a horse at the top of a high hill, and beside me was an angel of the Lord, who was also sitting on a horse.

We were overlooking a big valley. The valley was filled with the encampment of the twelve tribes of Israel. Each tribe had its own camp and its own signifying pennant.

Once again, I heard the shofar sounding, and the tribes immediately began dismantling their tents.

The angel said, "Behold, the whole house of Israel is preparing to move, for He (Jesus) comes soon!"

Amen.

12. OH, ISRAEL, OH, ISRAEL

[Note: I was given this song. I saw an angel playing a lyre, and I heard the angels singing these words. I could not repeat the melody correctly; however, the Lord gave my wife the melody line. When she sang it, I recognized it. "Yes," I told her, "that is it." -Isa. 60:1]

The angels sang:

> Oh, Israel, oh, Israel, thy Light has come to thee.
> > Thy beautiful Light has come!

> Oh, Israel, oh, Israel, thou shall not be ashamed.
> > My Grace has fallen on thee!

> Oh, Israel, oh Israel, thy Light has come to thee.
> > Thy Light has finally come!

I sang back to the Lord this response:

> Oh, Father, oh, Father, Thou art our Light.
Thou art our Beautiful Light!

> Oh, Father, oh, Father, we shall not be ashamed.
> > Thy Grace has fallen on us!

> Oh, Father, Oh Father, our Light has truly come.

Our Light has finally come!

Amen.

13. HEARKEN, OH, ISRAEL

Hearken and hear,

Oh, Israel!

The Lord Your God

Is one God!

And He is the Same,

Yesterday, and today

And forever!

Amen.

-Heb. 13:8

14. ISRAEL, THY LIGHT HAS COME

Prophesy to My people, Israel:

Israel, Israel, thy light has come. The time you have been held in derision is coming to an end.

Those who made you "a hiss and a byword" shall now be ashamed. For My Arm is about to be revealed from heaven, and all shall see it together, and all shall be in wonder.

Things that have not been known will soon be revealed.

Your time to shine, Israel, is about to dawn.

Prophecy, prophecy, prophecy is being fulfilled before your very eyes. Many will deny it, but others will sing in joy.

Now I Am going to change the culture of the world, for you have made a bargain with death, but now you shall see life. For I Am the Life and Light of the world, and the whole House of Israel shall be transformed.

Israel, oh, Israel, thy light has come. Let thy heart sing, and lift up thy voices together. -Isa. 60:1

MY TRUMPETS DECLARE, "I AM HOLY!"

PART III

PROPHETIC WORDS GIVEN

JERRY WILLIS

PROPHESY! PROPHESY!

15. I CREATED MY OWN FLESH

The Spirit says:

I Am Holy. And I sought to make a covenant with My creation, but they were not holy. So I created My Own flesh which was without fault. I made My covenant with Him, and He sealed it with His blood. So man is brought back into My presence. For when I look upon man, I see the Holy Blood, which makes man holy, and I Am able to see all My creation with love. So this covenant is holy, and *it shall stand forever*, for none can break this covenant which was sealed by the Blood of the Lamb!

Amen.

16. THE BLOOD OF THE LAMB

The Spirit says:

Just as I cast My rainbow in the sky to remind Me not to flood the earth again, so when I look upon flesh through the Blood of the Lamb, I Am reminded of the purpose of man. And I Am filled, without and within, with mercy and compassion for all who will believe in Jesus. For He was the Lamb sent to save, not to destroy, but to bring about love and peace.

Let not your heart be troubled. -John 14:1- Jesus will yet reign in Glory, for does He not reign in your heart at this time? So it will be for eternity for those who love Him.

Hear this day, and know that your place in this time is to share what you learn with others, until all hear the word and feel the love that only God can give.

Be brave through this time, My little ones. Do not be overcome by the world, but shine your lights brightly, for I Am that Light, and I will uphold you.

Trust in Me, and I will show you things yet not seen. Hear Me, and I will speak things yet unheard, for I Am

Alpha and Omega, the Beginning and the End. -Rev. 1:8

Amen.

17. HIS LIGHT IS COMING

The Spirit says:

Today the Lord is filled with compassion for His people. For too long they have lain in darkness. Now Light shall shine from heaven, and darkness shall flee. For time shall hasten.

Talk of it among yourselves, and uplift one another. Be blessed, My children, for your God loves you.

Amen.

18. THERE WILL BE WONDERS

Hear Me, oh, son of man:

There will be wonders, the likes of which have never been since the beginning of time. Fear not, for your Lord and God will protect His people! His love for those who will accept His Son has no end.

You have traveled far, but you have even more to travel. Learn all that you can, as quickly as you can. I have need of you. Fear not. I watch over you always.

Keep My commandments.[1] Stay close to Me, and I will be your Guide. You have seen only the tip of the iceberg. I have much love to give to My people.

Hear Me, those who are troubled: I will not depart from you. You who will keep Me close, I will uphold and support. Be not afraid for the things of this world. I have greater things to give you.

My love is endless, even as the heavens appear to you.

---

[1] The term "My commandments" is not talking about the Mosaic Law. Instead it refers to the teaching of Jesus in John 13:34, which says, "A new commandment I give unto you that you love one another as I have loved you…"

Love one another. -John 14:12- I will help you. Pray for one another. I will answer you. Always be open to My words. They will teach you much with My help. If you are troubled about any question, bring it to Me. I have the answer.

Remember, I love you all.

I came to save the world, not to condemn it. When in doubt, pray.

Amen.

19. TASTE THE SWEETNESS

The Spirit says:

My children, I want you to taste of the sweetness of this life, not the bitter, for the bitter must come, but woe unto he by whom it comes. For I have not sent My children here to suffer, but to learn at My Hand, not at man's hand. But some have chosen to listen to man rather than Me.

Bitterness comes from listening to man, and sweetness and peace and joy comes from listening to Me.

Amen.

20. BE OF GOOD CHEER

[Note: I was awakened at 7:30 a.m. by a still, small Voice.]

He said:

There shall be a major change in My people when they recognize that the Gift of Prophesy is *the pure love of Me*, the Christ, and receive it. They will begin to realize that whatever circumstances they are in, I Am still with them:

Rich or poor,

Strong or weak,

Sick or well.

I will break all bonds that hold them back from Me, and they will know that I Am God, that I have always loved them and will always love them.

Be of good cheer, My little ones. I come quickly in My own time, and you shall be able to see it with your own eyes.

Let no man beguile you, for as it is written, so shall it be. The first shall be last, and the last shall be first. -Isa. 41:4

Love one another even as I love you.

Amen.

Your weakness shall become strength at just the right time. And all things are as they should be. Let not doubt trouble you, for doubts shall be removed, and truth shall be given in its place. Many there are who shall learn doctrine, and many shall learn that they have greatly erred in their heart.

Those who hearken unto Me will be softened of heart, and I will heal them, for My Arms are extended still. Let those who will, come to Me. Come, for I call! Who will hear Me and open their hearts that I may have place in them?

My children will see and know that I have always taken care of them. Look to Me for your needs, for I will supply them.

This promise is to all that love Me, even unto the ends of the earth. It is My good pleasure to give to you the Kingdom -Luke 12:32, My children, and I delight in your love even as you delight in Mine.

Always look up from whence your salvation comes.

Do not allow the things of the world to overcome you, for they are temporary, and I Am Everlasting, from Eternity to all Eternity.

You shall hear of great troubles and all manner of tumult. Be unafraid, for it will not come near you.

It is the time of confusion for the unbelievers. Nothing will be right for them, for having natural eyes, they see, but being *hard- of- heart*, they see not!

All kinds of things must take place, for I have told and foretold them. But this is no consequence to those who believe Me, for they are Mine now and forever. But this time will be hard for all doubters and unbelievers. For this time is the last time I will call them.

Go now, Jerry, do that which I have and that which I will command you, My son. I love you. Peace be with you always.

Amen.

21. I AM GOD

Oh, hear ye! Hear ye!

All you souls of the Great I Am, hear and obey His marvelous words, which bring light to the darkness— which say to the worn and weary: Come to Me, and I will give you rest. -Matt. 11:28 Come, buy milk and wine without money and without price, for you have sold yourselves for naught. I have bought you back, so be of good cheer. -Isa. 55:1

Love one another even as I have loved you. Do good to all, even those who abuse you and accuse you. -John 15:12; Matt. 5:43-44

The day will surely come when all shall see the Light and know that I Am He. Talk of this to those whom you love and say, "I Am is the God of the whole earth!"

Amen.

22. LET ME KINDLE A LIGHT

Tell My people:

Know you not that I Am the Lord, that I Am a Sovereign God, and that I rule over all?

I treat all the same. I treat those who honor Me to be honored and all those who defile Me to be defiled. It is your choice that brings either honor or dishonor.

I extend forth My *Arm of Mercy* to all those who will obey My commandments.

And I say to all men everywhere:

Repent, and come unto Me while the Light still shines, and let Me kindle forth a light so bright that those in darkness cannot help but see. That they may know that I the Lord Am just and merciful!

Amen.

23. IF I AM THE CENTER

Oh, son of man, say unto this people:

To those of you who come to sing and praise and worship, this is good, for it is worthy. To those of you who come for healing and spiritual warfare, be encouraged, for this too is worthy.

I ask that you love one another as I have loved you, for I love each evenly the same. If I Am the Center, all things are as they should be.

You will and are doing a great work. It will affect many people if you will continue to love one another and stay focused on Me. The hand is not the foot. You need both.

Your enemy would have you function blind and unaware. Remember to allow no man to dissuade you from that which I would bless you with.

Be not afraid. I, even I, will fulfill all My promises.

 Amen.

[Note: Message given to our little home worship group. It is included for the encouragement of other small groups.]

24. KEEP YOUR EYES ON ME

Be not afraid:

Be not afraid even though the time will come when all those around you will be afraid. Even those who are closest to you will shake and tremble.

I say to you, "Fear not!" -Luke 12:32- Keep your eyes on Me, for I Am with you even to the end.

I have chosen you to stand strong for Me so that all those who are around you, who tremble and shake, may be comforted by your strength. For that strength is of Me.

Shine your lights brightly, My beloved children. Stand even as you are led in all things.

Amen and Amen.

25. I AM HOLY

The Spirit says:

I Am Holy. And I want you to know that I Am Holy, and I want you to worship Me.

Did My servant David, who was a man after My Own Heart, worship Me in solemn silence or in mourning? Or did he worship Me in song and dance? Did he not praise Me? Did he do everything according to man's tradition, or did he worship Me according to My Spirit?

You have the story of David. Read it, and then tell Me the answers to these questions. Understand My words. Soberness is not mournfulness. Holiness is not strict tradition. You are free in the Spirit as long as you follow Me. Be filled with joy, My children, for I love you.

Amen

26. VESSELS OF FIRE

[Note: I was sitting at our kitchen table, praying, when the Spirit of the Lord told me to write these words to His people.]

Let he who has ears to hear -Matt.11:15-, hear what the Spirit says to all:

My people have prayed and prayed for a long time. I have heard their prayers and cries. I know the long suffering that has been upon My people. I have now been *filled with mercy* for My people.

I have begun at this time to pour out My Holy Spirit unto vessels of My choosing. They will be filled to overflowing, and all whom they touch will be likewise filled with My Fire.

My Fire will start in this place and other places and will be an unquenchable fire upon My ministers and My people. They will shine both day and night, without ceasing, and none can withstand them or prevail against them, for they are Mine.

Fear not, for I Am with you always. Many there be who wished for these days and did not see them, and many prayed for them, but it was not the right time. But now is the beginning. I will fulfill all that I have spoken.

My love is endless love, My people. For those who hear, I will be their God, and they will be My people. -Lev. 26:12

I have given promises to those who will obey Me. Ask, and you will receive. Knock, and it will be opened unto you. -Matt.7:7

Come unto Me, My children. Reason with Me. Show unto Me your strong reasoning, and I will show you Mine. -Job 13:6

Blessed be the Most High God!

Amen.

27. COME TO ME

The Spirit says:

Let all who will come, come!

Let he who will not come be not compelled to come. But know this, there is still time to entice man to come, for the end is not yet.

Let your joy be full, and let your voices rise in songs of joy and praise to the Most High God.

This time is for peace, this time is for healing, and this time is for loving, for your God loves you so. Look up to behold the blessing of the Holy Spirit.

Times are changing, and there will be much unrest, but be not afraid of the dark, for I bring light to you. Heed My Counsel, and I will increase your faith and gifts.

I will give to all who diligently seek them. Do not say within yourselves, "How?" For you know how. Show yourselves to be My children by your actions. Do not be quick to judge, but be quick to ask of Me. Ponder My words, and in all your ways acknowledge Me. And know, that I, even I, will bless you.

Peace be with you always.

Amen

28. PUT YOUR TRUST IN ME

Tell My people:

I have been and I Am filled with compassion toward My children. I want you to know you are not here at this time by accident. You have a special purpose to fulfill.

This is a time like no other, and it calls for a people like no other—a people who have chosen to serve in a most momentous time.

The enemy is more daring as time moves ever forward, for he knows better than you the times.

I will continue to use any and all of you as you are willing.

Let not your hearts be troubled. -John 14:1 I Am with you always. Put your trust in Me. Look up, for I will be here. Let not your own wisdom overcome your spirit, for you serve the Most High God, and if you will depend on Me, you shall see that the wisdom of man is of naught.

Babylon is about to fall, and the world shall be in awe. But you, My children, shall be safe, for as I live and breathe, I will uphold thee!

Things will become clearer in a short time. Watch for the signs of My coming, and in a little while the cursing you shall see will become a blessing.

Those who believe in Me are Mine, and those who will not believe in Me are not Mine.

Fear not, little ones, you are special to Me. -Luke 12:32 I will be with you forever. My kingdom is coming. Be of good cheer, and bless one another in My name.

Even so,

Amen.

29. YOUR CHILDREN

Say to My daughters:

Those of you who have raised up your children in what you believed to be the right way, yet have seen them wander away from the gospel, away from their callings, and away from the teachings of Christ, I say: In those whom you have taught about Me, you have prepared the ground for My Spirit. The day is coming when I will pour out My Spirit, and then the changes in them, which you have hoped and prayed for but did not see, you will see.

The teachings of man are at an end. In a short time, My teaching begins. The fields of Zion will bloom, and your children will be called to a higher plane. Be of good cheer, for the Lord your God does recognize you and shall bless you always.

Amen.

30. COME AND FOLLOW ME

The Spirit says:

Fear not, little flock. Though you are small in number, I, even I, Am with you. I will lead you and add to your number as I see fit. If I Am at the Center, I will take care of you.

Endeavor to follow Me. Endure all things, and keep My sayings even as I have told you, for I will be with you forever.

Even so,

  Amen.

All things are possible with Me, and no good thing is possible without Me. Each one of you are precious in My sight.

I know many things that you do not know. Lift up your hearts, and be of good cheer. I Am even now working in your behalf. The world cannot hear or receive Me, but you are not the world.

Come, My little children, and follow Me. Believe in Me.

All that I have told you is about to come forth. I give unto you My love and say unto you, "You are Mine and have been from the foundation of the world."

You are here at this time for My purpose. And no man can dissuade you from that which you would do for Me.

Share your love with all that will let you, and always remember Me!

Amen.

My children, I would that you should understand that life, all life, is of great worth. You were not sent into the world to suffer as some believe. You were not meant to be miserable as many are. You are to have joy even as I had joy.

You are to embrace life and learn all that you can. Your place in My kingdom is assured if you follow Me! You will have great love and compassion on others if you let your light shine, for I Am that Light.

Love one another, and help one another to have joy in life itself. Let not the cares of the world unduly burden your soul.

I will not leave nor forsake you. All things are as they should be.

Amen.

You, by making Me the Center, become My friends, and friends are more than just known by one another. They are those for whom we would lay down our lives. Greater love has no man than that he lay down his life for his friends. -John 15:13-15 You may not at this time fully understand this, but you will as time rushes forward.

Put all your trust and faith in Me, for I have overcome the world. Peace be with you. My peace I give unto you. -John 14:27 As it was in the beginning, so it is now and forever.

Amen.

31. MY PROMISES ARE TRUE

Oh, son of man, take a pen and write these words:

As I live and breathe, says the Lord, My promises will be fulfilled. They are even now being fulfilled in the earth.

Fear not, for I Am with you. Many of My people stumble because of the world's teaching! Do not be swayed by the flesh. Listen to the Spirit. I give you peace through the Spirit.

Time is moving on towards the end, but it is not yet the end. All things work for good to those who love Me. -Rom. 8:28

Oh, My little ones, open your hearts to Me. Come to Me, repent of all evil, and I will cleanse you and make you whole. For I Am *Mighty to Save* and cannot be or do anything that is not holy. -Isa. 63:1

Rest on Me, and I will bring you great blessings. I chose you, My children, before you were born, and I do not make mistakes. Be filled with joy, for your salvation draws near.

Soon I will do something supernatural that will cause many souls to be freed from the grasp of My enemy, the enemy of the world, for the shaking has only begun and will get stronger.

I Am Alpha and Omega, the Beginning and the End. -Rev. 1:11 I came in the flesh and died for the sins of the world, and I Am alive forever more. Hear Me, My children, for the time is near.

Amen and Amen.

32. FOLLOW A HIGHER PLANE

Tell My people:

Allow not the blindness of others to affect you. Leave all earthly thoughts to follow a higher plane, for My thoughts are higher than your thoughts. -Isa. 55:9

If you call on My Spirit for guidance with a pure heart, you shall receive it. Pray often that you fall not into temptation. If you will do My will, keep your eyes on Me. Pay close attention to the task at hand. Leave all evil of the day to itself. Make your concentration be on things of heaven, not of earth.

If you keep My commandments,[2] I will be your Guide, and you will prosper. If you keep not My commandments and turn to your own way, you will surely fail.

My love for all My creation you know. What you hold in your heart for others is a key to what you seek. For I will not give to man to consume it on his lusts. What I do for one man, I will do for all, for all shall know that God is

---

[2] The term "My commandments" is not talking about the Mosaic Law. Instead it refers to the teaching of Jesus in John 13:34, which says, "A new commandment I give unto you that you love one another as I have loved you…"

God, and none shall have doubts.

I have blessings in store that you know not of if you will stay steadfast in your commitment to Me. For I Am unchangeable, and I work today as I have always worked: according to the faith and belief of man.

I know your fears and dread. Remember, I have overcome the world. They hated Me long before they hated you.

Oh, My children, I love you! Let each of you look into your own heart and so ask yourself if I Am not the same today as yesterday. Settle this question in your mind, and study and learn of Me. My yoke is easy and My burden light. -Matt. 11:30

Even so,

Amen.

MY TRUMPETS SOUND "WARNINGS"

PART IV

PROPHETIC WORDS GIVEN

JERRY WILLIS

PROPHESY! PROPHESY!

33. PROPHETIC WARNING

Prophesy to My people:

Warnings are being given to the world. It is time to repent of your iniquities and put your houses in order, for the Lord God comes soon.

Fear not! -Luke 12;32 Praise your Lord with all your heart, mind, and soul.

The time of the harvest is near. Remember Him in all that you do. His promises are true, and He will fulfill them all. All who have ears, let them hear. All who are blind will see the things which have been hidden from man. They will soon be revealed.

All who love the Lord are in His Hands.

Praise the Father, praise the Son, and praise the Holy Ghost, which is One God.

Amen.

[Note: Jerry responds to the Lord: "Heavenly Father, I am not worthy to bring this message to the people. I will as You will. My only desire is to serve You in the way You wish. I am

a sinful man and feel so humble before Your Holy Words. I praise Thee, Father, with all my heart and soul. How can I make Your wishes known? This is a task that a holy man should do, Father. I know, Father..."]

Warning given:

War will break out in the Middle East again. There will be a short time of peace to gather more people to the Lord. Hear ye My words, saith the Lord. I have seen all that goes on in the world.

I have laid down the foundation. You will know that I Am the Lord your God.

I have sent many messengers to you—some you did not recognize, some you scorned. Now for the last time will I send you a warning. Put yourself in My Hands.

Pray and watch that you will not be found lacking faith in Me. You must believe and receive My righteousness even in a world of unrighteousness. Let not a man be your guide. For I, Jesus Christ, Am your Guide. Love Me, and hold fast to My gospel. All will be as I have said.

Do not try to be like all others. Be as little children with open hearts, and the Lord will know.

Amen.

Fear not, for I bring to you love and peace. Though many things must take place that are unpleasant and many will reject the word, know and understand that this is the way things need to be. I Am in charge of all things, great and small. Continue to hold fast to My Word and My promises, and I will hold fast to you.

Lo, I Am with you always. -Matt. 28:20

Be not troubled for this world, neither seek after its riches, for they are a thing of naught and will soon pass away. Man will soon see that God is God, and My way will be the only way.

Blessed be the name of the Father and the Son and the Holy Ghost, which is One God!

Remember, while you worship Me one day, you have six more days to your week. I would that you remember Me those days also! Carry Me in your heart so that I Am never far from you, and I will carry you in My hands forever.

Amen.

34. THE LION SHALL ROAR

The words that I give you are of love and peace:

I desire that you call on Me for all that you need. All things are to work for your good if you will believe in Me. I Am He who has created you.

I love you and desire for you to spend eternity with Me.

All must either serve My enemy or serve Me. Remember, oh, remember, My words will bring life or death—life to those who hear or death to those who will not hear.

You find it strange that I speak more now than in the past? Fear not man who says it cannot be so. Why do you believe I cannot speak My own way? Those are strange thoughts indeed!

Hear Me, My children, for salvation comes. I Am He Who brings it with Me. Men do not control Me or own Me. I Am He Who is *no respecter of persons*. I will show My words to whom I choose, and they will write them.

Many things are soon to come, and you must be brave and fear them not, for I, even I, Am with thee. I will guide thee and comfort thee.

The lions shall roar, and men will tremble, but I will prevail! For I have already overcome the enemy. Soon they will be no more for a long time.

I command the times and the seasons, and My will is above all. I have chosen you. Who can take you from Me?

Amen.

35. THE GREAT DIVISION

The Spirit says:

There will be a great division among the people, because why would you give a gift to someone who does not desire it?

Time is coming for those who follow Me to separate from those who will not follow Me.

If your desire is to be a great leader, search your hearts, My people. Do you serve man or Me?

Lo, I Am with your always.

Be quick to bend your knee and slow to raise your voice. Hear Me now, for it is I Am. I Am will lead you to green pastures by still waters, for I Am the Good Shepherd. -Ps. 23

I Am Alpha and Omega, the Beginning and the End. -Rev. 1:11 I was born of woman. I suffered and died for the sins of man. I have risen, and I Am alive forever more! Even so,

Amen.

36. COME OUT OF BABYLON

The Spirit says:

My people, you must come out of Babylon! Seek only to follow the word of your Father in heaven. Do not listen anymore to the word of man.

The wisdom of what you seek is good. Your Heavenly Father has so much to give to you. This is the time for love. Because you seek, more will be given to you.

I know many of you are troubled. Do not be! Follow the narrow way. You are aiming high, and you will not be disappointed. Your Father will guide and comfort you.

The times to come will be difficult, but be not afraid. All the Father's promises will be kept.

Amen.

37. STOP RUNNING AHEAD

Tell My people:

The wishes of the men who lead you are not evil, but they are running ahead of Me, says the Lord. To you who are running ahead, I say, if you will pause, take a breath, and ask of Me, I will lead.

This is not a problem without a solution. I Am the solution, not man, nor the wishes of man. Ask yourselves some tough questions, and you will see for yourselves that the trouble is doing things in man's wisdom rather than Mine.

Listen closely and you will know that truth does not fail. If I call or speak, even all will see or know that I have done this.

I do not make mistakes. Man makes mistakes. All can be corrected if you stop running ahead of Me.

Man should realize that I Am still God, and besides Me, there is no other God!

Let not your pride rule you in this. Humble yourselves before Me, set aside your desires, and seek Mine. You may be amazed at what I do. But if you refuse Me, your decision may harm many people, not just you!

Remember, you are My servants. You are not rulers. Though many people give you praise, do not think higher of your place than you should.

Amen.

Surely things will be set right again, but not by man. For the Spirit of God brings peace and freedom. He wants you to stand for peace and freedom of the Spirit that He might take the proper place in your hearts.

Amen.

MY TRUMPETS PLEAD, "COME"

PART V

PROPHETIC WORDS GIVEN

JERRY WILLIS

PROPHESY! PROPHESY!

38. NO MORE PRETENDING

Tell My ministers:

This is the time that those who play at church, and those who believe that they have My power, must now bend their knee and bend their will to My will or they will be cast out forever!

There will be no more pretending to believe in things that they hold in no regard. For I have never ever given man My power to use over other men; but rather, to bring other men to repentance that they might be saved by Me.

My kingdom is coming, and every one of the churches which have placed worldly things (such as power, prestige, positions, political strength, and money) above Me, and those who have said within their heart, "Who sees us? For there is no God today! We are our own gods and set our own destiny," shall lament their thoughts. For the God Most High, who would desire to forgive them, can only forgive those who repent and come unto Him.

Thus says the Spirit:

I Am in the process of rising up a people, a people whose hearts' desire is to hear the words of the Lord above all things and who do not follow after another. For they will be My people, and I will be their God, and I will defend them and prosper them in My ways, says the Lord. And they shall never wander again. -Jer. 24:7

All these things are happening before your eyes. The way is becoming clearer each day to those who love Me. The *differences* between the groups I teach will all become fewer and their agreements more.

All things are as they should be. Look up, and know that I love you.

Amen.

39. YOU STAND IN THE DOORWAY

Tell My ministers:

Oh, My children, how far have you wandered from that which I have called you! Why are you so slow to hear? Why do you harden your hearts against Me?

I call, and none answer. I send messengers, and you reject them. Why do you believe you are better than your ancestors?

I have called you to be My servants, and you prefer honor from one another rather than My honor.

Come! Learn about Me from Me. None other can teach you.

You believe you are leaders of My people, yet you will not hear Me! You draw close with your words, but where is your heart?

Where is the healing of My people? You should be able to walk among My people and discern who it is that needs healing. And when you are praying for the healing, say not, "If God wills." You should already know His will.

Why do you attack any person who does not do exactly as you do? You are the same as the leaders during My days on earth. No one dares challenge you or you will destroy them if possible. Soften your hearts. Unstop your ears! Hear Me that I may heal you.

You stand in the doorway. Either come in or step aside. My work will continue. Even now I raise a people to stand in your place if you continue to reject Me.

My people, you are called to greatness. You are called to bring My love to My children. Be not slack. Repent, and come unto Me. Men will always reject truth. You are called to believe. Search Me out, you will find Me. Knock, and I will answer.

Amen.

40. OPEN YOUR HEART TO ME

Write, oh, son of man, and tell My people:

My ways are not your ways. -Isa. 55:8 If you will hear My words, then shall you be of My covenant. If you refuse, then shall you be cast off.

For a long time now have I held My peace. I have watched as man has turned this way and that way, being led as if by the wind! My beloved children, I call you to a higher plane. The things of this world are not of value.

If your heart be open and you hear, then shall you know that I Am. The peace of this world will soon collapse, and in its place shall be chaos.

Fear not, little children, hold fast to My Rod of Iron, My Word. All the promises shall belong to those whom I shall see doing what is written in the scriptures. For in the scriptures, this time is truly foretold.

Can you not look? Have you no eyes that you can see? Even now, My Holy Spirit pleads with man to accept the salvation of My Beloved Son, Jesus the Christ. The hour grows late, and I call.

Have you not ears that you may hear? I do not ask impossible things. With Me, what is not possible? Forsake the world now, and in your hearts hear only Me.

Little children, you are a delight to the saints on high if you will continue to ask of Me and keep My commandments.[3] Strive for holy things, and pray that you will recognize them as you see them. Lo, I Am always with you. -Matt. 26:41 Fear not those who doubt. Do not be mislead by poison tongues, which look for something wrong in everything.

Be obedient to My commandments. Pray often that you enter not into temptation. Small things bring about big changes.

I created this world to be a holy place and man to be a holy being. Though man has fallen, yet shall I not bring to fruition the things I have spoken?

You do not need to know all things. The things you need, you will know. I Am, yet some still deny Me.

When peace is taken away, fear will grip man. Know this, My children, I loved man enough to give My Only Begotten Son that He be born of flesh and blood and that He die on the cross, a sacrifice for the sins of man. If you will remember Him, how then can you doubt My love or that I will take care of you?

---

[3] The term "My commandments" is not talking about the Mosaic Law. Instead it refers to the teaching of Jesus in John 13:34, which says, "A new commandment I give unto you that you love one another as I have loved you..."

I have given, and will give to you, all the things needed in the very time that they are needed. Know, My children, that My love has no bounds. The world may desert you, yet will I not! As I loved men that you have only read about, so will I love you. Keep My Commandments.[4]

If any man shall doubt the truth of these things, let him ask in prayer of Me, and I will reveal the truth unto him. I do things not as you would have Me do. For My reasoning is strong. Come, let us reason together—any who will.

I set the cornerstone, and I create. All things are Mine, and I love them. I say unto all, now is the time and this is the place. Come unto Me and My Son Jesus and be with Us always!

Amen.

---

[4] The term "My commandments" is not talking about the Mosaic Law. Instead it refers to the teaching of Jesus in John 13:34, which says, "A new commandment I give unto you that you love one another as I have loved you…"

41. WORDS ARE POWERFUL

Tell My people:

You have heard the voice of an enemy come through a loved one of Mine. Now understand, oh, man, words are full of power—to do good or to do evil! Words said most carelessly can damage a soul.

You must learn when to speak and what to speak. There are times when silence is the most important of all. There will come a time when you will speak, and you will speak what you hear. I will lift you up, and you will be strong, though you believe you are weak. Your eyes are not fully open, and your learning is incomplete. Do not judge the things you hear and see by man's judgment. Your heart must remain on Me, and your eye must remain on Me as well. Though the law be right, remember My Spirit, and do what you see Me do.

Amen.

42. REPENT AND COME UNTO ME

Hear ye, son of man:

Oh, son of man, many of those who lead thee cause thee to error. Until My ministers come to Me on their knees with full desire in their hearts, thus shall it be.

Those who would be king men, and those who believe they have authority, forget themselves. They forget where the authority comes from. If you believe your authority is from an organized church, you are part of the world. If you believe your authority comes from Me, why do you follow those who you know are in error? Why do you not ask of Me first, not last?

I say unto you, repent and come unto Me. Place Me at your head, and I will lead. Follow no more the ways of man. Learn from on high by prayer and faith.

Oh, son of man, tell My people they are without excuse. They give their support to things they know are against My scriptures and speak not. I know their hearts, and I know their fears, for I have lived among man. I say unto them: Support no cause that goes against My Word, for all My words will be fulfilled.

You are much loved, My people. Come back to Me, and allow Me to lead you. Fear not, for My Arm is not shortened, and I Am not late! I Am *Mighty to Save*, and I come quickly. No man shall know the time but the Father only.

Remember, men seek after their own power. You must not become part of this.

If My ministers seek Me not, then follow them not! If they stray from My Word, stray from them. I have chosen some of them, but not all, for man has chosen some. Look to My example and judge.

I Am Alpha and Omega, the Beginning and the End. -Rev. 1:11 Learn of Me from Me.

Amen

Oh, son of man, do you suppose in your wisdom that I Am not able to lead? Do you suppose that I Am somehow less than I Am? Do you suppose that I need your money and buildings to accomplish My work? Use righteous judgment, Oh, son of man. All these are needs of man.

If thou wilt follow Me, understand that you will not be well received of men. Understand that I Am not as man perceives that I Am, for your wisdom is foolishness before Me. If man rejects you, remember he rejected Me first. If he accepts you, he will accept Me. My will is that all those that the Father has given Me be not lost. The Father has given all judgment into My Hand. As I see, I judge, and My judgment is just. Place your trust in Me, Oh, son of man, for I Am with you always.

Even so, Amen.

If any man will ask the truth of Me, I will show him. Come, let us reason together, and I will show you My strong reasoning. -Job 13:6 For My Arm is extended still toward man. If any will come, let him come. Come to the Rock of Salvation. Come unto the Water of Life. Any who hear, come, and I will give you rest. My invitation is to all.

Even so,

Amen.

43. MY WORD BECOMES FLESH

Tell My people:

The wicked have filled the world with the abomination of evil. They teach the young even before their birth. The constant exposure to violence and filth of all kinds has its effect.

My Word must become flesh!

Oh, My people, weep not for the wicked. For the truly wicked know what they choose. Pray for the souls of men. Have your hearts ready, for the Bridegroom comes in His own time.

Be not partakers of the world's ways. I have given you the path to follow. Trust your Lord.

Be of joyful hearts. For verily I say to you, salvation will come to those who wait on the Lord God.

Feast on My Word and pray. Keep Me in your heart. For I Am He who laid the foundation of the world, and I Am even He who saves.

Amen.

44. I AM NOT A MAN

The Spirit says:

Oh, son of man, as you seek to worship Me in Spirit and in truth, so shall it be! If you would worship Me in truth, you must know the truth. So as you desire, My Spirit will enlighten.

Know now, oh, son of man, that any agreement between you and Me is a binding agreement. It is everlasting. The same as the covenants I made with your forefathers.

Know also that there are great rewards for faithfulness and severe penalties for unfaithfulness. I Am not a man that you may deceive Me with your intellect, for I gave you your intelligence.

Look deep into your hearts and know your own purposes. If truth is what you seek, you will have it from this very hour. I Am pleased to give it to you. For My love for you is endless. I seek those of truth to worship Me.

Fear not! I will be with you. Do not take your eyes from Me, and I will not take My Eye from you. Blessed are you if you do this.

Take no heed of the size of your group. It is wisdom in Me that it be small as you put your foundation in. I follow not the patterns of men, but I Am the True Creator. I can increase or decrease as suits My needs. Be wise stewards, and keep all My Commandments.[5]

Never have I set one man above another in My Church. If I give My Spirit to rule in My Church, then your unbelief is all that would keep you from the Holy Spirit, for I Am no respecter of persons. I have given authority to My ministers to feed My sheep. I have placed My Spirit upon them for this purpose.

It is the faith of My people that increases or decreases the Spirit. It is the responsibility of My ministers to be watchmen and shepherds of My sheep. I love My people and My ministry alike. If they all remain faithful to Me, their reward is great! All who seek shall find, and blessed are they, for they will know the truth.

Amen.

---

[5] The term "My commandments" is not talking about the Mosaic Law. Instead it refers to the teaching of Jesus in John 13:34, which says, "A new commandment I give unto you that you love one another as I have loved you…"

45. STOP YOUR FUSSING

The Spirit says:

I have poured out My blessings on My people, and they would rather fuss and fight over trivial things than accept My blessings!

Amen.

46. I CHOOSE WHOM I WILL

Oh, son of man, hear My words today:

Your judgments are not just, for you judge according to your traditions. Have I not told you, "Ask and you will receive?" Yet you persist in your own will.

I have sent people to you and have given you guidance and will continue to do so. It is wisdom in Me that all is not revealed at this time. You shall return to your studies and your prayers and your supplications to Me.

I choose whom I will. For it is a small thing that I use whom I use!

My ways are not your ways, and My thoughts are not your thoughts. -Isa. 55:8 If thou would do My will, make peace your guide.

Reject not My messengers, for I shall be among them. As I have given to you, so shall I give to all who will hear My Voice. Blessed are they who hear and rejoice at hearing.

If you love Me, keep My words. Place no man above another man. Neither should you say in your heart, "He loves one more than another." Neither should you say in your heart, "He loves one more than me." For this is foolish pride. I call all men to Me. He who rejects me, I withdraw from.

You are to forgive all. I have given all for you, and I will fulfill My words.

Oh, son of man, time is short. I come! Hear now My words.

Amen.

Your sins are forgiven you.

Abide in My Love always.

Amen.

47. THE ALABASTER BOX

[Note: "And being in Bethany in the house of Simon the leper, as He sat at meat, there came a woman having an alabaster box of ointment of spikenard very precious; and she brake the box, and poured it on His head." -Mark.14:3, 8 "She has done what she could: she is come a-fore hand to anoint My body to the burying."]

I struggled with this scripture about the woman anointing Jesus. I had belonged to churches where men were the church authority. I knew the account was true! It was right there in the Bible that I had been reading for years.

It shook up all kinds of man's traditions that I had been taught even as a child. As always, I reasoned and discussed it with my wife, Vivien. It was something new, shown to her by the Holy Spirit, when she found the scripture in which a woman anointed Jesus. -Mark 14:3-9 She and I together wanted the truth. We realized that if a woman could anoint Jesus Himself, what could she not do?

We also discovered that Phoebe was a woman, who was a pastor, who "patronized" Paul: "And I am introducing our sister Phoebe to you, since she is also a minister of the congregation in Cenchrea, so that you would welcome her in the Lord as befitting the saints, and you would stand by her in whatever matter she would have need of you, for she has also become a patroness of many, even of me." -Rom. 16:1NMB "Literally, Phoebe is a woman set above others." -NMB, page 1503, footnote 3

Then we saw Priscilla and Aquila working as a married couple-team. "Listing Priscilla first indicates a greater ranking for her in Paul's mind." -NMB, page 1503, footnote 3

"You must greet Miriam, who labored much, teaching among you. You must greet Andronikus and Junia,* my kin and my fellow prisoners, who are prominent among the apostles, and they were in Messiah before me." -Rom. 16: 6-7, NMB *Junia was a woman. -NMB, page 1503, footnote 6

We were surprised by all of this and wanted the Lord to confirm it. I was still pondering, struggling with this concept, when at the breakfast table during a quiet spell, the Lord gave me the following, message:

The Lord God said, "If the intent of a deed is holy, then the deed is holy. If I have inspired the deed, then it is holy. You need not confuse the precepts of men with the Holiness of God. For My ways are not your ways, and My thoughts are not your thoughts.

Give unto man that which is man's and unto God that which is His. For there is no difference in My sight between one creation and another. Both man and woman have I created, and I love them both. And if their intent be to serve Me, what I have said applies to them all. For I Am Holy, and all things holy come from Me! And thus it is,

Amen.

Recently, I received another message on this subject. The Lord said the following:

I have shown plainly the hypocrisy of man when Judas said the ointment could have been sold for much and given to the poor. -John 12:6-9 Judas never knew where she got the oil. I said to him, "For you have the poor always with you," knowing full well it was not the poor that were foremost in Judas' mind.

Likewise today, there are many who would stop the work that I want done because it is not done the way they think it should be done. If a woman is called of Me, speaks of Me, praises Me, and holds Me up, why then do men say this cannot be?

Did I not say to the disciples, "Leave her alone, for she has done a good work?" I had apostles there, and I could have had any one of them anoint Me, yet I chose a woman who loved Me—a woman, lowly thought of by many, and a woman I had forgiven much.

I washed My apostles feet. This woman washed My feet with her tears and dried them with her hair.

I read the heart. I Am not a respecter of persons, but men are. Even My apostles showed signs of being respecters of persons.

Look up, My children. Look up, for you neither know who will be in heaven or who will not. Rely on Me. Look upon Me. Do not rely on men but upon My Spirit.

That little alabaster box was a woman's way of showing her great love for Me. She acted on the influence of My Father. Be not quick to judge, but be ever quick to believe, for all good things are influenced by My Spirit. Things are as they should be.

Amen.

48. THE STORM IS COMING

[Note: This morning Vivien and I were worshiping in the Spirit. I saw the trees shaking, and the ground began to shake like a great earthquake. As I felt the ground moving beneath my feet, fear began to arise within me. An arm appeared, then I saw a second arm appear, and they wrapped around me.]

Then I heard these words:

Be not afraid. The storm is coming. Yes, the storm is coming, but all those who love Me, I will wrap in My Arms. They need not fear, for I seek to save, not to destroy!

But I must shake away all things that keep you from Me so that your hearts I may fill—that I may fill them with My love, which is endless. Then you will be free to do My work, for I will work in you and through you in the midst of the most horrendous storm.

You shall stand like an anchor when you see that all about you is fear and dread. You shall say to that *spirit of fear and dread*, "We bind you up and cast you back to the pit from which you came! For the Lord our God is greater than all, and you shall not remove His people from His Hand!"

All things are as they should be. All things will be as I have said, for I Am Alpha and Omega, the Beginning and the End -Rev 1:11, and beside Me there is no other. No, I know not one. -Isa. 45:22

I will move faster and faster, for the end is yet to come.

Then I saw Him stretch forth His Hand and say:

"My Arms are open still, but time grows short! Come to Me quickly, My children, that I may gather you unto Me, that I may have you for My children, and that I may protect you and bless you with the Kingdom that My Father has given Me. Thus saith the Spirit."

Amen!

49. A WARNING

[Note: This message given to me was followed by a vision of "My Garden."]

Go to, son of man, and write what I tell you, for I Am Alpha and Omega, the Beginning and the End. -Rev.1:11 Write and say to My people:

I, even I, have sent men and women among you to call you to repentance—to call for you to return unto Me. You say, "We have not gone astray. We are following Christ." I say, "You have stopped your ears, blinded your eyes, and hardened your hearts that you cannot hear or see or love whom I send you."

Some of My ministers have been led into error and have in turn led My people into error. Now I will tell you what I will do. I will call, and My people will answer. Those who refuse My call are not Mine.

Hear Me, oh, My people. Unstop your ears, open your eyes, and open your hearts that I may enter, for I will raise a people whom I will command. I will not cast any away who come to Me.

Oh, son of man, tell them of My love. Tell of My joy at

their repentance. Tell of My Garden and its delights. If you will ask Me, I, even I, will tell you of these things. I Am Alpha and Omega, the Beginning and the End. -Rev.1:11

I know the hearts of My people. Ask, and you will receive. Knock, I will open.

Fear not what others say. Fear God only and serve Him

I know those among you who lie down at night, thinking all is well in Zion. "We serve the Lord, and all is well."

What of those who you will not hear? What of those who speak truth? What of those who speak in the Spirit? You hear and listen politely but are so comfortable in your own ways. So I tell you what I will do. I will make it so that you can no longer be comfortable—so that you will have sorrow, so that you will know fear and hunger and thirst, and you will know that I alone Am God!

Oh, My people, do not turn away your hearts.

Hear My call.

Come, let us reason together.

Come

To a knowledge of truth.

Come!

Be that for which you are called.

Come!

Cast off the shackles with which you are held.

Come

To a knowledge of peace,

Come

To a knowledge of love,

For I Am love, and I will guide you

If you will turn aside from the ways of man.

Call on Me; I will hear.

Come back, My beloved, to the garden.

Amen and Amen!

50. TELL ABOUT MY GARDEN

A VISION

[Note: Much of this vision is symbolism, which is explained throughout and at the end of the vision by Christ. So be sure to read the full account. It will be a blessing to you.]

The Lord said, "Tell My children of My Garden!"

I inquired, "Lord, how am I going to tell them about Your Garden if I have never been there?"

Immediately, I was transported in the Spirit to the Lord's Garden. I relate it this way:

I was walking in a dark, green forest. I was following a Lamb. He was the cutest baby Lamb I had ever seen. He was pure white. He had dark eyes that glistened. He gave light, and He was the only Light in this place. I never took my eyes from Him. I knew it was Christ, and I just wanted to hug Him so close!

My spirit was like that of a child.

All at once we came to a bright clearing. It was the most beautiful, peaceful place. I do not have the words to describe it! I looked all around, and the dark forest seemed to surround this bright area. I saw the Lamb leading, so I followed Him.

I became aware of the sweet smell of flowers in the Garden. I saw all kinds of flowers. They were perfect in color, shape, and size. Some of the flowers I had no knowledge of and had never seen. The smell was so sweet, like a giant potpourri!

Then the Lamb headed into a different area of the Garden. I followed, led by an irresistible urge, like a child following a beloved pet. I felt like a child, exploring a wonderful new world.

There were all kinds of familiar fruits there, such as grapevines with grapes as big as silver dollars that melted in your mouth. I also saw unfamiliar fruits as well. I tasted of the fruit, and it was good!

I looked and saw many small animals joyously playing together, no longer predator nor prey. I knew this was a special place.

A young doe came over to me and without speaking, asked me, "Are you going to stay here?" I wanted to so very much, for I have never felt such unimaginable peace and joy. I knew, however, that I would follow the Lamb!

The Lamb led me, and I followed to what appeared to be the center area of the Garden. There I saw a man standing by a tree. It was an enormous tree, dwarfing all other trees. Its fruit was unfamiliar to me.

The man called to me and said, "Come, come, taste of the fruit." I tasted it, and it was delicious! It filled me with ever more joy, even the joy of the soul.

I recognized the man as a prophet of God. He had long gray hair and a matching beard. His eyes were bright and shining. He wore a robe like the Jews of biblical times. He was not a tall man, maybe 5' 7" or so. His countenance glowed. He was so full of love.

This tree I partook of is always in season, and its fruit spreads unspeakable joy of the Lord. Birds of all kinds nest in the branches of it and sing the most wondrous songs to the God of creation.

I became aware again of a smell that was sweet, like cinnamon or vanilla, although a bit different.

The Lamb led me to a place, a special place, where I saw what appeared to be smoke from incense rising up. This was where the smell came from. The Lamb said, "These are the prayers of My children."

Then I saw a pool of water so clear and so deep. It seemed to have no bottom. I knew immediately that it was the *Water of Life!*

I became aware of many happy animals in this section of the Garden also. Can you imagine scratching a 1000 pound grizzly bear as if he were a teddy bear? The grizzly laughed and said, "Let's wrestle!"

He swung his huge paw, with claws the size of my fingers, at me. He would surely tear me apart! Yet when his paw hit, it hit me with all the force of a cloud.

These animals were more mature than those I first saw, and I wondered why. And as quickly as I questioned, the answer was given. The creatures of the Garden grew from one area to the next area.

The greatest surprise I received was to be given an instant insight: The animals were not animals at all, but people! My spiritual eyes were not allowed to recognize these as people, so I was shown all of them as creatures. Only the prophet by the tree appeared as a person.

The inhabitants of this Garden were so full of love for one another in this beautiful Garden!

Then the Lamb led me to the "entrance" of His Garden.

I noticed a veil between the garden and a path that stretched beyond the horizon. The path outside of the veil was lined with people of all ages trying to get to the Garden. The people wore scarred and tarnished armor. Their shields were bent. The people, themselves, had many scars and wounds of all kinds. Some had lost limbs, eyes, and other body parts. They had suffered much!

Jesus alone controlled the gate and greeted each one. As the suffering people came through the gate, they were transformed from pain into profound joy! I saw them as creatures when they entered the Garden.

I saw other people outside the veil. They laid down their broken swords and their bent shields. They took up new weapons and went back to the fight—the war raging beyond the Garden. They went willingly to sacrifice for others. Their one wish was to help souls find their way to the path which led to the Garden.

I turned and saw the Lamb ready to lead me to another corner of the Garden. There I saw full grown animals: leopards, lions, tigers, bears, boars, and eagles. They were grazing like cattle, and they had no desire to harm one another or to get gain from each other. They were quiet and loving. The Lamb said, "These are the nations of men when they will be healed!"

"Now go to, son of man, and tell My people of My love. The flowers are the good seeds men should plant. The fruit trees are what grows from the good seeds, for when good is mature, it becomes fruit. Tell of My Garden!"

I wanted to stay forever in His Garden, but I knew I must do as He asked, for I am a bond servant of Jesus the Christ forever!

Amen.

MY TRUMPETS ANNOUNCES "MY STRANGE ACT!"

PART VI

PROPHETIC WORDS GIVEN TO

JERRY WILLIS

PROPHESY! PROPHESY!

51. JOY AFTER BIRTH PAINS

Tell My people:

These are birth pains, the beginning of the "Great and Marvelous Work and a Wonder." -Isa. 29:14 For I have told you before that all things that can be shaken must be shaken, not only in the earth this time, but also in the heavens. For when the shaking is done, that which is left will be standing on a firm foundation, for I Am that Foundation!

Behold, My Word cannot fail. Be not afraid, for fear makes you shake. I have given promises, and My promises are true, for My Word cannot fail!

Look upon Me, and know of a surety that all that believe and are baptized shall be saved. Let those things of the world come what may, for your place is assure if you will stand on the foundation that I have given you. So be it.

Amen and Amen.

52. REMOVING THE SCALES

[Note: I was saying to my wife Vivien, "You and I did not know 20 years ago what we now know about Christ." We marveled with each other about how the Lord had taken the two of us down this path toward Him. Then Christ entered our conversation, which was perfectly normal for Him to do.]

Jesus said:

For two thousand years I have tried to remove the scales from man's eyes. But some are stubborn about having their scales removed, and some are afraid of the unknown. I show them *Who I Am* as the scales get thinner and thinner. For as the scales become lighter and lighter, they begin to see Me more and more!

Amen.

53. EVIL VS LIGHT

Speak these words unto My people:

Because I appointed certain men unto destruction in the time of war and the leaders of the peoples of the earth refused to destroy evil for their own purposes, the evil, which is strong upon the earth, has been covered and allowed a foothold to trouble My people.

I will bring this evil to the light that all may see that the God of the whole earth lives and is the same today as yesterday and will be tomorrow.

For the day comes that all they who serve a false god shall look up and howl at the sky. For the evil they have done shall fall upon them when they shall not believe it, for I know their plan, and it will come to naught.

Fear not, for the Lord Your God doth protect His Own. Put your trust in the True and Living God.

Thus it is.

Amen.

54. EVIL WILL BE DESTROYED

The Spirit came upon me, and I heard His Word:

The time shall come when all that is evil will be destroyed. For I Am coming to the earth I created, and My children shall be under My Wings. For it is My desire to save the whole world. But I will save only those who will, for I Am Holy, and My thoughts are holy.

All those who will not believe My words shall perish. For no evil shall remain. I wish to make all things good that My Kingdom shall remain forever.

Amen.

It shall happen when they think not. It shall happen when they say, "All is well." It shall happen, for I the Lord have spoken it!

Amen.

Oh, My little children, be not afraid, for I will protect those who are Mine and will not destroy them. I know how to be good to My children. I have always been good to them, for they hear My Voice and follow Me.

It is the enemy that has brought suffering and illness to this place.

Come to Me with all your might, mind, and strength, and I will strengthen and heal you. Keep your heart soft, My children, even towards those who accuse and abuse you. They are lost at this time, even as some of you were lost in the past. Remember it does not yet appear what will be, but when it is here, it will be wonderful. Go in peace, and be of good cheer, for I love you, now and forever.

Amen.

55. GOD NOT BE MOCKED

A VISION

I saw a huge building. It was biggest at the bottom where the congregation sat. Then it had a small second story built over that for the ministers of higher authority. Another smaller story was built over the second story for an even higher ecclesiastical office, and so on for several layers.

The highest authorities saw members begin to leave the lowest level. Those members leaving made holes in the side of the lowest level while getting out, but those in authority would just send someone to patch up the holes so no one could see that some had escaped. But soon the lowest level came out in larger numbers, which caused the top layers to tumble and to be destroyed!

Words given to me were: *God will not be mocked!*

56. BLOWING ON THE COALS

The Spirit says:

They will say it is an evil wind, but I tell you it is of Me. I will blow on the coals and blow and blow until they become hot, for I Am tired of lukewarmness! And I shall blow until it is aflame and burns hot and bright, for it will be of Me. Be not afraid of the blowing. Calm yourselves, and trust in Me. I will separate and separate until all that is left is the love of Me.

Amen.

57. A DAY REMEMBERED

Prophecy is being fulfilled even as you speak.

For a millinea I have watched and waited for My children to reach out for peace. But they have used their own minds. They have used their own wills. They have done that which I have not asked them to do!

However, evil will not overcome My children, even if I have to open the *Windows of Heaven* to save them.

Every word in Scripture I have told and foretold to My children. Even though I received wounds in the houses of My friends, I have not forgotten them.

The world is moving at a fast pace. Delusion has descended on the hearts of men. I will open the eyes of those who are deluded that they might see the truth. Those who seek after Me will be free of the delusion and bonds of the enemy.

This is not the end but the beginning of a strong wave of My Spirit. My Light is coming to destroy the darkness, and that Light is Me. Love is coming into hearts where it has not been before. My Spirit is going forth among My people at a pace never before seen on earth.

Revivals have been in the past and faded away. A new revival is coming! As the ocean tide raises so will the waves of My Spirit. It has already begun, wave upon wave, time after time, like the ocean currents. These ocean waves cannot be changed by man. Neither can man stop these waves of My Spirit.

Stand for Me, My children, and in your beliefs in Me. Stand firm in your love for Me as I stand firm in My love for you!

Let not the fears in this world keep you occupied. Look up. Look up in joy. Realize you are nearer to Me today than you were yesterday, and you will be nearer to Me tomorrow.

Prophecy is being fulfilled. All things whatever are in My Hand. I love you, My children. My love for you will not change.

Amen and Amen.

MY TRUMPETS ANNOUNCE "MY NEW WORK"

PART VII

PROPHETIC WORDS GIVEN

JERRY WILLIS

PROPHESY! PROPHESY!

58. MY TRUMPETS ARE SOUNDING

My trumpets are beginning to sound!

There are many that will not hear. Let those who have ears to hear, let them hear. -Matt. 11:15

For My trumpets are beginning to sound!

Many have looked forward to this time and have not seen it. But you will see it. You live in a momentous time. Let he who has ears to hear, let him hear.

For My trumpets are beginning to sound!

And they sound in My power. I wish to gather you as a hen gathering her chicks.

For My trumpets are beginning to sound!

Things are happening very fast, faster than you can imagine. You need to be prepared. Share this with as many as you can

For My trumpets are already blowing!

Not the same trumpets that will blow when I, Jesus Christ, comes but trumpets of the voices of My people arising! The Spirit of Elijah has already gone forth.

Ask, and it shall be given to you. Seek, and you shall find. Knock, and it shall be opened unto you. -Matt.7:7

Amen.

59. A NEW WORK

"Open your heart," says the Lord.

I Am about to do a new work that will change the way men see Me. I Am the same today as yesterday. All things are in My Hand, and all is as it should be, for the world is My creation, and all mankind was created by Me for My pleasure.

Because of the fall, many do not understand their relationship with Me. But soon they shall see Me in a new light. And when this occurs, their hearts will either be softened through My *Gift of Repentance* or they will be hardened by their own carnal thinking.

For I Am God, and beside Me there is no other. -Isa. 43:11

Hear My Words today, My children, and come to Me with a broken heart and a contrite spirit that I might bless you with a gift beyond your wildest imagination. -Isa. 57:15 For eye has not seen nor ear heard the glorious things that I have in store for the children who hear My Voice and obey Me.

Be of good cheer and be encouraged, for I come quickly, and none can take you away from Me.

Amen and Amen!

60. A NEW WAVE

Tell My children:

Oh, My beloved children, I would that you would love one another, for all love comes from Me. I Am the Great I Am, Whose Voice shook the earth. And Whose Voice will shake not only the earth, but it will shake the heavens also!

The time is coming when every knee will bow, and every voice will confess that Jesus is Lord. -Phil. 2:10

Know now, My children, that I Am in all things and will protect those who love Me.

These words are all in your scriptures, but I tell you of them that you might believe that I Am He that speaks to you.

I Am beginning a new wave of My Spirit upon the earth. It will be unlike any before it. For My Spirit will change hearts and minds that you, My children, shall be freed from the things that bind you from Me. For I Am and will bring freedom to your Spirit that you can call on Me and I will answer you if you will hear and obey Me.

I will lead you to do things you will not think possible, but all things are possible with Me. Only believe.

The Kingdom is yours. It is My good pleasure to give it to those who believe. Never will I repent or turn from you, My children. Come to Me with open hearts and minds, and I will fill you with My Love that you will be able to share My Love with others.

Be of good cheer, and know that the Great I Am has blessed you forever.

Amen and Amen.

61. THE COVENANTS WILL BE

Hear Me, My children:

Oh, My people, I call you to a higher level of worship. You must put your trust in Me and realize that all things are Mine.

I know your fears. Be of good cheer and rejoice, knowing you are closer to the *Day of Reconciliation*. For whatever occurs in this physical world, I have already overcome, and I have promised to take care of you.

This is all a matter of necessary happenings in the order of the universe. Your joy should grow. Do not let despair steal the truth from you. Now things that were wrong will be made right, and love shall grow rather than hate. Your ways are not My ways. Evil is not defeated by return of evil but by love, My love. I come quickly though no man knows when. Take joy in My Glory as I take joy in you. For yours is the kingdom if you endure. No matter what happen, let love be always in your heart, for love is from Me. I come quickly though no man knows when.

Hear Me, oh, My people. I Am aware of your every thought. Some please Me, and some do not. I call you to

169

higher thoughts and higher planes—always to bring you who will come closer to Me.

The world is full of sad and tired people who have lost their hope and need more love and light. It is not like men think it is. No, it is the power of My Spirit that must prevail, for all goodness is contained in My Love.

I will fulfill My promises, and they will come that you shall see My Salvation. And all mankind, every man, woman, and child, shall know that My Love is endless.

Oh, My people, love one another, take care for the sick, feed the hungry, and clothe the naked. Pray that ye be not tempted, for the time grows shorter, and soon the covenants will be.

Even so, Amen.

If anyone would ask the truth of this, bring your reasoning to Me, and I will show you what is true. I Am the Beginning and the End, Alpha and Omega. -Rev. 1:11

In love and peace,

Amen.

62. MAN'S GREATEST ACHIEVEMENT

Hear ye, saith the Spirit:

[Note: One Tuesday, early in the evening, I put on the movie, "Apollo 13," and began to watch it. The Lord suddenly poured out His Holy Spirit on me to an extent that I have rarely experienced! I was so overpowered by the Holy Spirit that I felt like I was only about two inches tall.]

The Lord asked me, "What do you think is man's greatest achievement?"

I answered, "Man landing on the moon? I don't really know. Was it winning World War II against all odds?"

The Lord answered, "That was done by My Hand." The Lord added, "All the greatest achievements of man, from the very beginning until now, will be as nothing in the face of what I Am about to do. None will be able to deny that it is I who does it! It is because there are people who still love Me that your country is not destroyed. There are many who still love Me, and I will not allow the evil to overcome the righteous."

Amen.

63. A VISION OF JESUS

[Note: My wife Vivien was going to take Communion one morning. The Lord quickened my heart to desire to have the Sacrament with her. As we were partaking of the Lord's Sacrament, I had a vision of Jesus Christ.]

Jesus was beautiful and majestic! The people were falling down before Him. They were ashamed because of their sins. They expected Him to judge them and condemn them for their sins. But there was no condemnation in Him, only love!

Amen.

64. THE STRONG MEN

The Lord God says:

Muster the *Strong Men* of My House, for they have taken an oath, and I call upon them now that they honor that oath, regardless of the condition they find themselves in. For I, the Lord of Hosts, say, "I come quickly, and the strong men of My House must stand against evil, whether it be outside or inside My House!"

All the things that I have spoken shall come to fruition. For unlike man, I do not speak lightly. I choose My words with care.

All things are as they should be, for I the Lord Am forever! Stand strong in your belief in Me, and I will stand strong for you, and the day to come will bring you no harm.

Amen.

[Note: Man or men designates mankind. This refers to strong believers.]

65. HOLY WORSHIP

VISION

The Spirit said, "Look!"

And I beheld a group of people who were assembled to worship. I saw that their minds were in different forms of thought towards God:

Some were thinking of the church and how beautiful it was.

Some were thinking of how great the spoken word was.

Some were thinking about after church.

Some were asking God about their children.

Some were looking to the church leaders to bring them the right attitude, but the church leaders were so involved with their office that they could not hear the Spirit.

I wondered how could worship be done with so much distraction, and why would this be so?

The Spirit said, "Look, for even the humble followers are taught by the precepts of men."

"Can no one then worship?" I wondered.

The Spirit said:

Man must put down all his assumptions and the traditions that are of man. He believes he knows of himself, but he does not know.

The leaders of this day are no different than yesterday. They must bend the knee and call on Me for Divine intervention, with full purpose of heart. They cannot be caught up in the traditions of the world any longer. Worship is a holy thing that can only be done from the heart. Love is the answer and the key, for I so love man.

I have not changed, and I am the same today as yesterday and will be the same tomorrow. -Heb. 13:8 If you will open your heart and call on me, I will guide you.

Your love of Me is what makes you happy and secure. I have called on My ministers many times to repent, but they cannot hear, for they are dull of hearing. They have hardened their hearts towards Me by placing others in My place.

I am a jealous God. Thou shall have no other gods before Me. -Ex. 20:5 Come back to your First Love, and I will come to you.

Fear not! -Luke 12:32 All things are as they should be. If it were not so, I would have told you.

Keep an attitude of prayer in your heart. And I, even I, will be your God, and you will be My People.

I know your thoughts and wishes even before you speak them. Men will always use those who are humble, but endure to the end. The reward is great!

I Am Alpha and Omega, the Beginning and the End, even Jesus Christ. -Rev.1:11 The Same Who was born of woman and suffered and died for the sins of man, and I Am *alive for evermore.*

If you would worship Me, put all things aside.

Do not think of your position.

Do not think of your differences from others.

Do not think of the world.

Think of My love for all—how much one soul is worth to Me! Do not allow anything to push that from your heart. And you will find a blessing in your worship and prayers that you have not seen in a long time.

Amen.

66. ONE DROP OF JESUS' BLOOD

VISION

[Note: Preceding this short vision, I was told by the Lord that only one drop of Jesus Blood was beyond any earthly value.]

I saw a balance scale.

On one side, the scale was completely weighted down by a single drop of Christ's Blood. Men were carrying in many, many huge chests of emeralds, diamonds, rubies, and gold. They were loading them on the other side of the scale.

All the precious jewels and gold could not cause the scale to budge. All the treasures of the world put together could not compare to *One Precious Drop of Christ's Blood!*

Amen.

67. HE POURED OUT A DROP

VISION

I saw gatherings of people in their churches all over the earth. I saw them sitting in their pews. They had many different thoughts and ideas about God, worship, doctrine, and all things pertaining to the Spirit. But they listened to men. They called them by many titles (pope, priest, elder, pastor, etc.), and the people heard what they had to say. And the people worshiped everything—the building, the books, each other, the men—everything but the Spirit of God.

They believed what they received was from the Spirit of God because it made them feel warm and fuzzy inside, but it had nothing to do with God because it was a "religious spirit."

Then I saw an angel in the midst of them. The angel was floating in the air above the people. He had a vial in his hand. He poured out a drop from the vial, and the liquid went up to the ceiling instead of landing on the floor of the church. Then it began to spread out to the walls, down the walls, onto the floors, up the pews, and onto the people.

I was told that the liquid from the vial was a pure drop of the blood of Christ. As it spread on to the people, they began to open their eyes, soften their heart, and say strange things like, "This is the God we worship. This is the true Holy Ghost. For we have been deceived, and we were blind, but no longer! For this is the Spirit of the Most High, even Jesus Christ, and Him will we hear Him and no other."

They began to throw down the false things that held them and to break the shackles. The broken shackles fell away. This same scene spread to each new place where the angel poured out a drop, and it spread to the whole world!

This is a true vision given by the Most High God. For His people shall be loosed from those things which have been taught by the precepts of men. Their understanding will increase, though the wisdom of the wise has perished. God will now do His Own Work! And no man shall take credit, for it is of God, and all shall see. They will not ask another, "Is this of God?" For they shall know.

68. HEALING RAIN

VISION

My wife Vivien and I were visiting ministers at a weekend retreat. During one morning's prayer service, I looked over the congregation and wondered if something was wrong with my eyes. It looked like rain was falling upon the people. I rubbed my eyes and looked again. It still appeared to be raining. Then I looked outside to see if it was raining out there, but it was sunny!

Once more, I looked back out over the congregation, and I could see the rain coming down upon us. That is when I understood what was happening. The Lord had opened the heavens and was pouring down His love upon us.

Later on, I heard a song on a CD, which I had never heard before. It is called, "Healing Rain," by Michael W. Smith. Vivien. I love the Holy Ghost, so let it rain, and let Jesus Christ Reign!

69. LOVE IS THE SEED

The Spirit says:

Oh, My people, why is it that you are so troubled by the things of the world? Is it not written that a seed must die before it can produce?

Why can you not understand that this life is fleeting and of no worth? That which is to come is glorious! Can you not see that your love is seed? And it will multiply even as I have said, "Some a hundredfold, some sixty, and some thirty?" -Matt. 13:8

Do not be quick to see the mote, but rather watch for the beam, lest pride enter in. -Matt. 7:4 Endure to the end and thou shall be saved.

Amen.

70. SEEDS OF LOVE

VISION

The Lord said, "Reach out and take My Hand. I Am going to take you on a journey."

[Note: I said to Vivien, "I'm going to lay down a little bit." Vivien said, "Hey, I'll take a nap with you." As soon as we laid down on the bed, I told her, "The Lord just said to me, "Reach out and take My Hand. I Am going to take you on a journey." I immediately fell into a peaceful sleep that lasted for about two hours. My body was asleep, but my spirit was taking a journey! This is the vision as I recounted it to my wife for recording.]

After Christ took my hand, I was walking with Him at the base of a mountain. I had never seen a mountain that high and I said, "Wow!"

Then we were immediately at the top of the mountain. My senses were strange as I was not cold, even though there was plenty of snow and ice. Neither was I tired. Then without a word, I knew that Jesus wanted to talk to me. So I sat down and leaned against a big rock. Jesus sat down across from me. He sat higher than I was, for He sat on top of a rock.

Jesus said, "Hold out your hand."

Then when I obeyed, He poured out many small seeds into my hand. They were glowing with light. He continued, "You are to plant these seeds of My Love into the hearts of men."

Jesus added, "I have things I want to show you, and you will not understand them for a little while, but as time goes on you will understand."

Then Jesus and I were in a valley. Everything was beautiful, expansive, and big! Each vegetation was rich, dark green, and very lush. Every seed that fell upon that ground immediately began to grow!

Jesus had me part the grass so I could see the soil. The soil was dark black topsoil. Rich, rich! You could actually smell its richness. Jesus told me this valley represented the hearts of men.

Next He took me from the valley to a rich, lush jungle. It was wonderful. I saw all these carnivorous beasts: bears, lions, tiger, leopards, and wolves. They ran to Jesus with so much love, gentleness, and sweetness. They recognized who He was, and they behaved like house pets, lavishing their affection on Him.

He said, "The day shall surely come when they shall not hurt nor harm in all My Holy Mountain, for they shall be full of the *Knowledge of God.*" (Not intellectual knowledge, but spiritual knowledge—the knowledge of Who and What Jesus is! -Isa. 11:9

Then the Lord repeated that the seeds He gave me were for planting His love into the hearts of other.

End of vision.

THE TRUMPETS ANNOUNCE MY MARRIAGE

PART VIII

PROPHETIC WORDS GIVEN

JERRY WILLIS

PROPHESY! PROPHESY!

71. THE BRIDE OF CHRIST-PART I

VISION

I saw the Bride of Christ standing by a pool of water. She was filthy, and the robe she wore was filthy. Then I saw her stretch out her foot to put her toes into the water.

The vision ended.

[Note: I was given to know that the water represents the Holy Spirit.]

72. THE BRIDE OF CHRIST-PART II

VISION

[Note: Vivien and I were listening to Christian music and worshiping the Lord. Suddenly, I had another vision of the Bride of Christ.]

I saw the Bride of Christ walk to the pool of water and put her toes into it again. But this time, I saw her step all the way into the water. Then she began to wade out deeper and deeper into it. As she did, the filth on her body and robe was washed away. The water got so deep that it covered her head. I feared as I watched her that she might drown. But immediately, she began to rise up and out of the water, which was now dirty.

As she rose up, I could see that not only was she clean when she came out of the water, but she also had on her beautiful bridal gown. While she was rising part way out of the water, Jesus came to her and took her hand. Then she rose all the way up.

Jesus had His beautiful wedding garment on as well. Together they walked on top of the water to the other side of the pool, prepared for the Wedding Ceremony.

73. THE BRIDEGROOM COMETH

VISION

[Note: In the afternoon my wife Vivien and I were sitting at the table reading and discussing scriptures.]

Suddenly I heard these words:

To the Bride of Christ I say,

Throw off those rags;

Throw off those filthy garments;

Throw off those things that have kept you bound!

Cleanse yourself;

Anoint yourself with sweet smelling oil;

Put on thy wedding dress, My bride;

Adorn thyself with thy jewels;

Put on thy wedding veil;

Prepare thyself,

For the Bridegroom comes soon!

Then I saw this beautiful bride emerge. She was the most beautiful bride I had ever seen. On her head was a headpiece made up totally of pearls. She had cleansed herself in a pool of water, representing the Holy Spirit.

The sweet smelling oil stood for the praises and prayers of God's children. She wore two earrings and ten rings on her fingers. Both earrings and each ring had a different gem in it, which stands for the 12 tribes of Israel.

Those things which have kept her bound are a myriad of things—including man's doctrines, traditions, and man's reasoning. That list could go on and on.

End of vision.

74. I WILL CHERISH HER

VISION

I saw the Bride of Christ again. I saw her veil hang down to her shoulders. The top of the veil was encrusted with large pearls. She wore a shawl (cloak) with seven Eyes. These represented the Seven Spirits of the Holy One.

Around the girdle of the bridal dress was a white velvet rope for a belt. The belt ends had tassels, representing purity and the chastity of the virgin.

The four to five inch wide antique lace border at the bottom of the dress had little loops with a little tiny bell in each loop. The bells tinkled so lightly, so beautifully, as she walked. They represent the Bride's Holy Worship of the Bridegroom. And the Spirit says:

This is My Bride, and I will cherish her forever. This is what I have longed for from the beginning, for now has My Bride been cleansed and prepared to be with Me for eternity. Never again shall she hear a harsh word from My Mouth!

75. THE MAJESTIC GROOM

VISION

[Note: While Vivien and I were worshiping Jesus and while listening to the song, "Shout to the Lord," I had a beautiful vision.]

One of the verses of the song says, "The mountains will bow down and the seas will roar at the sound of your name."

I saw the most beautiful sight:

The Lord was wearing His golden crown and walking through the midst of the mountains, which were bowing down to Him. The sea waves were crashing. Jesus was so magnificent! He walked along in complete calmness and peace. I had never seen Him so magnificent as this. Jesus does reign!

Amen.

76. A SHAFT OF LIGHT

One Friday evening, while two people were praying during a worship service in Grain Valley, Missouri, I saw a vision:

I saw a shaft of light come down slowly from Heaven. As it got closer, I noticed that angels were very quickly coming down in a spiral. When they came close to the earth, they scattered in all directions. After they dispersed from the shaft of light, I saw that in the midst of the light stood Jesus! Because the light was so bright around Him, I could not really see His face. Then the vision quickly faded away.

Amen.

77. HE DOES EXCELLENT THINGS

[Note: One day while driving to our bank, Vivien and I were singing and praising the Lord. A voice spoke to me.]

It was not a voice I recognized, so I asked the question, "Who are you?"

There was a short reply: "I am an angel of the Lord."

So I continued to question, "Do you believe that Jesus was born of a virgin, came and died for the sins of man, and that He arose on the third day and is alive forevermore?"

The angel replied, "Yes, I know that He is God, and all things that He does are excellent. For God created the heavens and the earth. And are they not excellent in your eyes?"

"God created man and breathed into him, and he became a living soul. And is that excellent in your eyes?"

"He came to the earth in the flesh, and He died for the sins of man. He took all of sin upon Himself that man might not die but have eternal life if they would believe in Him. Are these not excellent things in your eyes?"

"For God is so full of love for His creation. Now what say you, is this not excellent in your eyes? Blessed is the Most High God."

Amen.

78. MRI VISION OF JESUS

VISION

[Note: A few years ago, I suffered a mini stroke at Nevada, Missouri. I was asked by my physician to undergo an MRI.]

When I went to the clinic, the technician asked, "Are you claustrophobic?"

I told him that I had never been afraid of tight places.

"Well, you are going to be cramped inside of this," he said, referring to the MRI machine.

"However," he continued, "There are mirrors that you can look at and see me. The machine is noisy. If you become afraid, tell me immediately, and I will take you out."

It never occurred to me that I could become afraid.

The technician put me on a table-like skid, and then into the machine I went. I could see him, just as he said, and could also hear the noise.

I became a little bit sleepy, so I closed my eyes. As soon as I did, an awful feeling of dread and fear came over me.

Quickly, I opened my eyes and was about to call out, "Get me out of here!"

But then I realized that I was alright after all and had nothing to fear. I asked myself, "Why are you afraid?"

I called silently to the Lord. As quickly as the fear came, it left. Calmly, I closed my eyes, and when I did, I was immediately taken to a place that I recognized was an outside stage. There were a lot of people there, but only One was standing and speaking to us.

I knew immediately Who He was and thought, "What's happening here?"

Thinking I must be asleep, I quickly opened my eyes. But indeed, I was completely awake and back inside the machine. So I closed my eyes again, and instantly, I found myself back with the people who were gathered around Christ. I relaxed.

But I listened intently to what He was saying:

"Do you realize that when they reject you, they reject Me?"

Jesus told us, "If they hate you, it is because they hated Me first! Do not be afraid of them. Follow Me." (John 15:18)

Later I was taken out of the machine, and all was well. I have been asked by others what Christ looks like, and I tell them, "He looks like no one, yet He looks like everyone."

This experience was humbling—one which made me look at others much more compassionately.

I know He lives, for I have seen Him, and He loves His creation more than we can ever imagine!

Amen.

79. THE BATTLE

VISION

[Note: I was walking in the Holy Spirit when I had this open vision.]

In my vision I walked into an expansive valley. Suddenly, there appeared a strange panoramic sight. There was a host of silver knights with battle armaments. On the opposite side of my view was a huge mob of black knights driving gigantic, horrendous monsters ahead of them. These monsters were destroying and chewing up people. There was carnage everywhere.

The silver knights came to battle the black knights. The black knights were full of hate and cheered whenever a silver knight fell. On the other hand, the silver knights were filled with God's Love. They were sad to have to destroy the black knights. The silver knights' swords had lazier-like beams coming out of them. They were straight beams. The enemy had lazier weapons also, but the beams were crooked. The battle ensued but was no longer visible to my sight.

[Note: The vision I saw was a battle between God's Army and the adversary's army. It was a battle between Light and

darkness. The Lord explained that the monsters stood for demons of hatred,demons of fear, demons of addictions, and more of the spiritual demons and enemies of man.]

80. THE COMING OF CHRIST

VISION

I saw an angel of the Lord. He stood before me, and He spoke to me saying, "All that you have seen must shortly come to pass. Write it down now lest you forget!"

So I wrote the following vision according to the commandment given to me by the angel:

In a blink of an eye, I saw all things that are already prophesied in the scriptures. The earth opened her mouth and swallowed many ships and many people. The mountains fell, and the rocks were broken. Cities were burned with fire, and some sank into the sea. Others were buried in the earth.

But the more righteous part of the people was spared. Those who were spared were not without sin; however, they were willing to obey the Lord and His commandments,[6] and they did not throw stones at His prophets.

---

[6] The term "commandments" is referring to loving God and others.

The wailing of the people hurt my ears, so terrible was their pain! Many had lost their family members and friends. Some had lost their husbands and some their wives. Some had lost their children and some both. Horrible was the anguish and suffering of the people.

But how *just* are the judgments of the Lord, for the people who were lost had refused to accept the Grace and atonement of our Lord. Oh, that they would repent before this day comes! As surely as I live and breathe, it will come. The earth will change her face at the coming of the Son, even Jesus, and the holy angels.

And I heard the angel say to me, "The time is now! For surely man has transgressed all the Holy Words of God Almighty, and the blood of the saints and prophets comes up before His face and accuses them day and night. God has held His peace for a long time, but no longer!"

My soul cried out, and I was afraid at a level I had never experienced. I believed that I was going to be wiped from existence because of my sins and iniquities. The angel said, "Fear not, for I show you what will surely be."

And I saw, after the thunders and lightning and fires, that there was indeed a vapor of darkness that descended over the whole earth. So thick was it, that I could feel it. I was so frightened that I begged the Lord not to show me any more of the vision for fear that my heart would fail.

The angel said again, "Fear not, for this must be."

Then I heard a Voice speak to all the people. They all stopped their groaning, and the Voice said to them, "I will dry your tears, for the time of My coming is at hand."

The darkness parted, and I saw a beam of light, small at first, which grew and grew until the whole earth was lit by the brilliance of the Light.

And the Voice said, "Let the Millennium begin."

Immediately, the heavens opened, and I saw uncountable numbers of angels and saints coming with the brightest light—so bright that I could not look. But I knew that Light was Jesus Christ in all His Glory. And I testify to this in His Holy Name.

Amen.

Now I understand what I never understood before: Mankind's purpose is to become sons and daughters of our Lord and Savior, Jesus Christ. The Same Who was born of woman and suffered and died for our sins. The Same who arose from the dead and now sits on the Right Hand side of the Father. I know this to be true, for the Spirit of God testifies to me that it is true!

Amen.

ABOUT THE AUTHOR

"I am only an ordinary man with an extraordinary God." This was one of Jerry Willis' favorite sayings. Another favorite saying of his was, "It's all about Jesus!"

Jerry was baptized, attended, and served in three different traditional churches during his lifetime. Their doctrines are different from each other. Before Jerry went home to be with the Lord January 29, 2015, he no longer belonged to an organized religion. Instead he belongs to Jesus.

We who loved him as husband, father, grandfather, brother, and friend mourn the loss of this wonderful man and prophet of God!

After being baptized in water in 1993, Jerry was not expecting the results which followed his baptism of the Holy Spirit. After he received it, he could barely walk back to his chair. For three days after that experience, he was still *walking in the Holy Spirit*. He saw open visions, a few which are included in this book. The Lord called him to prophesy to *His People*. Again, Jerry said that it was not about him, but it was all about Jesus!

After Jerry left organized religion behind, guided solely by the Holy Spirit, Jerry and Vivien hosted a worship group. Jerry was the pastor. It was a tremendous experience until it ended several years later. Then the Lord sent Jerry and Vivien to do hospital ministry instead. Together they formed the "Jesus, King of Glory Ministries," and "Jesus, King of Glory Publishing Co."

Jerry always repeated the fact that he learned more from the Holy Spirit's teaching than from anyone else!

Jerry and Vivien both earned Doctor of Christology degrees from an accredited Bible school, "The Spirit of Truth Institute."

Through praise, Jerry encouraged and embraced worship.

All the gifts of the Holy Spirit were sought after and enjoyed by him! His wife still enjoys these gifts today.

As mentioned before, Jerry and Vivien served as volunteer chaplains for the local hospital. They both have given prophetic ministry and prophetic blessings in their home. Vivien continues to minister anywhere she is called. Jerry was always delighted to share with others the wonderful spiritual relationship each person can have with Jesus.

Jerry had a special calling of his own. He was indeed a *trumpet* sounding out words of warning and words of God's love for His people everywhere, regardless of their doctrines, traditions, or where they are in their walk.

This book is for all those who thirst for the Word of God —for those who need to hear their Heavenly Father say, "I love you" or "Be not afraid!"

www.ingramcontent.com/pod-product-compliance
Lightning Source LLC
Chambersburg PA
CBHW060236050426
42448CB00009B/1473